The Single Guy's Guide to Getting Your Shit Together

By Andrew Ryan

www.singleguyguide.com

Legal Notice

Disclaimer

the information in the Ebook as an alternative to advice from an appropriately qualified professional. If you have any specific questions about any psychiatric or medical matter you should consult an appropriately qualified professional.

If you think you may be suffering from any psychological or medical condition you should seek immediate professional attention. You should never delay seeking medical advice, disregard medical advice, or discontinue medical treatment because of information in the Ebook.

TABLE OF CONTENTS

CHAPTER ONE

Have you ever had that sobering moment of clarity when your life suddenly makes perfect sense? When you finally start to take charge of your life and turn your luck around?

It's a very emotional, uplifting moment, when you finally decide to become the hero in the story instead of the victim...

I kind of imagine it might be accompanied by triumphant piano chords, overlooking a majestic ocean view...

Well, for me, my dramatic moment of clarity came in a dirty, shit stained dunkin donuts bathroom.

It was the morning after my 30th birthday.

There I was, staring into the grimy bathroom mirror in disgust..

The front of my shirt was soaked in sweat and reeked of alcohol. The back of my shirt was flecked with brown and red puke stains.

I steadied myself against the sink and tried to remember what happened the night before...

At 11 pm I remember talking to this chubby, obnoxious girl, because she was the only girl at the bar who actually wanted me...

Around 1 am, we went back to her studio apartment... but some other weird couple was already there, in bed... so she dragged me into her walk-in closet...

I didn't even want to hook up with this girl... I was drunk as a skunk and just going through the motions, unable or unwilling to just stand up for myself and say "I don't want to do this"

A few minutes later, I got what was coming to me...

She pulled me close to her in the cramped closet, tried to kiss me... then wound up puking down the back of my shirt, and crying tears of shame onto the front of it...

I tried to comfort her, then my instinct for self-preservation kicked in, and I bailed on little miss "closet vomit"...

I remember going back to my brother's place... but he couldn't hear me knocking to get in, so I passed out on his front porch...

I woke up at 7 am with mosquito bites all over me, and stumbled down the block to this shitty grocery store with a dunkin donuts inside of it...

And now, there I was in this dirty bathroom, dizzy and hungover, trying desperately not to puke into the sink...

This is how I started my thirties. SUPER exciting, right?

But I guess there's some weird, twisted part of me that can still laugh in these situations... and I needed to laugh at something that morning, even if it was just laughing at myself and how pathetic I was.

So I walked out of that bathroom, dizzy and tired, and I sent my brother this picture...

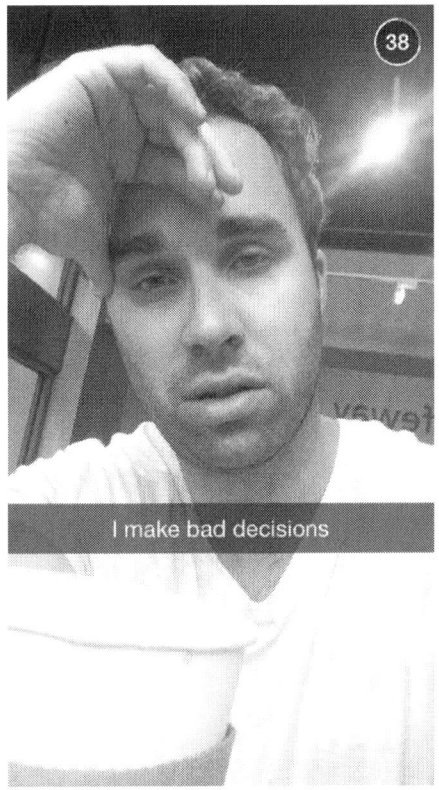

I make bad decisions

Look at that guy. Look into his eyes.

Those are the eyes of a guy who does NOT have his shit together!

And you know what, it's moments like that, when you're shaking and shitfaced in a grocery store at 7 in the morning, and you've got little stains of puke and tears all over your shirt...

It's moments like that when you really can't lie to yourself anymore.

Fortunately, I can laugh at myself now. But at the time, I honestly felt like my life was over.

I was 30 years old and I felt like I had nothing to look forward to, no reason to get up in the morning, and nothing to feel proud of.

Now, I could handle the hangover... that was nothing.

But what I couldn't handle - what I REFUSED to handle any longer - was the sickening feeling in my stomach that I was failing at life... failing to live up to my potential...

I wasn't even coming close, man.

If the guy I was at 20 could have seen me at 30, he would have been so disappointed...

I could no longer ignore that urgent, desperate voice in the back of my head, telling me to WAKE UP... that life was supposed to be BETTER than this. That I could be doing so much more with my life... and I wasn't.

Have you ever felt that way too?

Have you ever felt disgusted with yourself... or with the people close to you? Have you ever felt frustrated with how your life is turning out? Like you're getting older so much faster than your goals are getting accomplished?

Have you ever woken up to find yourself living a life that does not even remotely live up to the expectations you had when you were younger?

Have you ever felt like deep down, you are squandering your potential as a man... that you have so much more to offer, and to give... but instead you're simply SETTLING for an average life, with average girls who do not excite you in any way...?

And most importantly...

Has any of that ever made you feel angry?

I hope so. Because you know what the alternative is? Feeling sorry for yourself. And I think we both know that's not gonna fix anything.

Look, when I was standing there in that dirty ass bathroom, I suddenly knew exactly what needed to happen. I looked in the mirror and I told myself...

You did this to yourself, man. You got here as a result of your bad decisions, and your limited way of thinking.

But that also means...

That if you got yourself into this mess, you can get yourself out of it too.

3 years later, sitting here writing this book, I'm so excited to tell you... I found my way out.

I stopped feeling sorry for myself, I got my shit together, and I created the kind of life for myself that I used to daydream about... a life filled with incredible abundance, of money, friends, and yes... amazing, sexy, beautiful women.

Not only that, but I work for myself, my time is my own, and I'm surrounded by positive, like-minded friends who challenge me and support me every day...

And - get this - I've made such a dramatic turn-around in my dating life, and had SO much success with the opposite sex, that guys now seek me out for advice and guidance.

In fact, for the past 3 years, guys from around the world have crammed thousands of dollars a piece into my pockets to teach them what I do best:

How to attract astonishingly beautiful women, radically expand your social circle, and become the most valuable, confident, charismatic version of yourself... the guy you know you're meant to be... but who you're NOT being right now.

If you're anything like most guys I've worked with, at least 1 of these challenges may describe you:

You feel lonely and "in a rut" with your dating and social life... like Bill Murray in groundhog day, living the same boring day over and over again

You often feel like a deer in the headlights around attractive girls... and your fear of rejection has you falling flat in conversations, running out of things to say, and getting ignored...

You're tired of going on date after date, just to have the girl suddenly get bored with you and stop texting back...

You feel like you're never gonna be good enough to date the women you really want... you're too old, too short, too fat, too quiet, too shy, too boring, too poor...

You're struggling with addiction to pornography and it's making you a shell of your former self... the only women you interact with are pixelated fantasy girls inside your secret digital harem on the internet

You feel powerless and invisible around women, and people in general

You've been taken for one too many rides on the emotional rollercoaster of dating... where you feel validated every time your crush texts you back, and you feel like a worthless piece of trash every time she doesn't

You're fresh out of a breakup or a divorce and you're struggling to get back in the dating game...

You can't seem to get over "that one girl"... no matter how hard you try and how many opportunities with other girls you let slip through your fingers...

You're trapped in the "friend zone" with a girl and you would love to have a sexual relationship with her... but she doesn't see you that way

You're a virgin and you have little to no sexual confidence or experience... and the thought of getting older and older without losing that v-card is starting to terrify you..

You're doing "okay" with women but you know, deep down, that you've been settling for the girls you know you can get, instead of the girls you really desire... and you have no clue how to step your game up and start dating the really attractive, high quality girls that actually excite you

You've had a hard time making friends and creating a fulfilling social life since college ended (or even during college)

You have plenty of friends, but they don't challenge you or excite you, and you're longing for a better life, but they are all perfectly content with staying the same

You're sick and tired of getting ignored, walked on, talked over and chosen second

You feel like you're getting older and your window of opportunity to meet a quality woman is passing you by, and you feel powerless to change that

----

Look man, if even ONE of those things comes somewhat close to describing you, then I want you to know two very important things...

1, you're in the right place, and you're not alone. In fact, you're in the majority - most men struggle with these things, but very few have the balls to step up and change their situation, so I applaud you for that, and for picking up this book.

2, I've been there, and I do feel you.

Look man, I don't know you personally, but I'd bet that if you're reading this book, there's at least one BIG thing holding you back from true success in your dating and social life...

Maybe it's one specific girl you can't get over, maybe you're in a rut and it's hard for you just to talk to people, or maybe you're just sick of feeling average and you're dying to level up in life...

Whatever the case, I guarantee you there's at least one piece of wisdom in this book that will prove to be the missing puzzle piece for you, probably many.

Put them all together and you've got one hell of a life.

This book is what I wish someone would have given me, all those years ago.

It's not a book of tactics... you can get plenty of tactics in my training programs, my Youtube channel and my newsletter, which you can join for free at www.singleguyguide.com

This book is here for a more important reason - to make you THINK differently.

You won't find any "do this, say that" type of advice here. This is a book of wisdom.

These are the biggest breakthroughs and revelations that change your entire personality and way of thinking, almost overnight.

Not the little "baby steps" like "make better eye contact" and "push your comfort zone a little bit every day."

No, these are the big paradigm shifts that obliterate the very idea of "comfort zones", radically alter the course of your entire life, and forever change the way women look at you, starting today.

This isn't gonna be corny "just be yourself" advice your mom told you, and it's not the cheesy "be a better man" advice you see in men's magazines either.

It's also got nothing to do with corny pickup lines or sleazy PUA tactics.

I'm gonna tell you exactly what no one else is telling you...

How to get so many girls chasing you at the same time, there might as well be a waiting line to date you.

How to skip the "small talk" and boring dating BS most people have to go through... and get women turned on and seeing you as a sexual option within the first few minutes of meeting you.

How to create a fun, exciting social life from scratch, where you're surrounded by amazing people and you're never bored... even if you're new in town and you don't know a single person yet...

And most importantly, how to actually LIKE yourself... so much, that women stop what they're doing and stare at you when you walk in the room.

If you're a single guy and you're not living the life you want right now, then this is exactly what you've been looking for but haven't been able to find in other so called "dating advice" books.

A simple, no BS guide to getting your shit together.

Let's do this.

CHAPTER TWO

Here's a powerful piece of advice that no one ever tells you in the beginning...

Now that you're taking massive action and getting your shit together, you need to start being very selective about who you take advice from.

For example, when I first started telling my friends I was studying psychology and dating advice to get better with women, many of them said things like...

"Why would you do that? It's not that hard to meet girls, just go out to the bars, get drunk and hit up the dance floor"

When I quit my high paying engineering job to become a dating coach and travel the world teaching this stuff at bars and nightclubs across the US, Europe and Australia, they said things like...

"Wow, that sounds so easy, your coaching clients must all be huge losers - you should bring me along to the next event, I could give them so many tips"

(yeah, I'd like to see them handle the pressure of approaching girls while 10 guys watch you and judge your every move)

Girls always tell me - "why don't guys just ask girls like me for advice? I can tell you everything about what girls want from men, they want to be treated like a queen, and asked out to dinner, and sent flowers at work, etc..."

And most of all, whenever I'm around insecure people, they almost always say things like "oh, so you're a pickup artist, I know all about you - you must manipulate women, right?"

Or, girls will say "so you're just running your routine on me? Is this what you say to all the girls?"

Look, I've heard these skeptical, fear-based remarks so many times, I've come to expect it, and either ignore it, or have fun with it... You should too. It's standard human nature - people ridicule what they don't understand.

But this is a good thing for you.

When you start to change your lifestyle and make big moves for yourself, getting a little push-back from your friends and peers is a sign you're doing something RIGHT.

You're changing, they're staying the same. You're facing your fears head-on like a man, they're still avoiding them. Your success triggers their insecurity. Expect this to happen. It always does.

But trust me, when they see the kind of girls you're suddenly going out with, and the parties you get invited to, the adventures you're having... hell, just the big goofy grin on your face because you're finally stoked to be on your way UP in life... their snarky comments quickly change to envious stares.

So promise me you won't listen to any naysayers or pretenders, deal?

See, most people go their entire lives not even knowing that super successful people can give them advice and help change their lives...

I donno, I guess they think self-improvement advice is corny and uncool...

So instead, they take advice from whoever is around them - and that's almost always people who only have mediocre success with their own life.

At worst, they listen to people who have already given up… people who quit on themselves long ago.

If you've ever seen (or been) a guy in a lifeless, passionless relationship, you know people "give up" on themselves all the time.

Just because you're single, and they're married or have a girlfriend, does NOT mean they know more than you about women. If that were true, married people would never get divorced.

But when the divorce rate is over 50% in the US, you can bet that most men are making big mistakes in choosing a wife, and it's because they never took the time to understand themselves, understand women, and actually have a wide range of OPTIONS to choose from.

Let me tell you a little secret that only the most successful guys can tell you - the secret to getting the hottest girls isn't about learning the best lines and tricks and seduction techniques…

The secret is in rapidly expanding your OPTIONS.

When you don't have options, you end up taking whatever girl you can get, and then holding onto that girl for dear life, for fear of losing her and never getting anyone better.

You might even end up marrying that girl, not because you're madly in love with her... but because you're getting older, she's putting on the pressure, and you'd rather just go along with it than face the loneliness of being single again...

When you don't have options, you obsess over every little thing a woman does, and chase her for validation like a lovesick puppy dog.

When you don't have options, you resign yourself to a life of scarcity, insecurity and fear, and sadly that's the life of the majority of men on this planet.

But when you DO have options, everything changes for you, and the more options you have, the faster and more dramatic the change.

See, women are highly intuitive. And when you have lots of other women in your life, they can tell.

They pick up on the fact that other girls like you, and it makes them want you ten times more... without you having to DO or SAY anything different.

Man, if you get this one concept, you're gonna be set for life. I mean this.

With lots of options, you can choose to date as many girls as you have time for, or you can choose to date just one, but the most important thing is - you actually HAVE the power to choose!

But you can only choose when you have OPTIONS to choose from.

As you progress through this guide, and through your journey, I want you to keep this in the forefront of your mind.

Don't seek to meet 1 girl at a time... seek to meet as many as you can, as fast as you can...

Seek to create an abundance of options.

And ignore the people who call you a "player" for talking to multiple women. Those people are only judging you from a place of fear and scarcity.

The truth is, sleeping with lots of women doesn't make you a player or a bad guy... unless you are intentionally lying and deceiving those women, which I will never advise you to do.

For example...

When I'm single, and I wanna date as many girls as I feel like, do you know what I say to every girl I'm seeing, right at the beginning?

"Hey, I think you're amazing and I'm really enjoying this, but I just want you to know something - I'm not looking for anything serious or committed right now, and I want you to know that up front, because I don't want to date anyone if they're not cool with that. If you're not cool with that, I totally understand, and I won't waste your time. Are you cool with that?"

9 out of 10 of them say "Yes, and I'm glad you said something because I actually feel the same way."

(yep - girls can be liberated and "date around", too... get used to it!)

You don't ever have to lie or be a player to get lots of girls, man, Honesty will liberate you, like you wouldn't believe.

A man living a life of confidence and abundance doesn't ever think about lying or deceiving anyone, because he never has to lie to get what he wants...

But sadly, this is the main reason most men never undertake this journey - because other people judge them to be sleazy for even thinking about it...

And if you think dating lots of women is sleazy, and your goal is to be a good person, then you'll never allow yourself to become a "sleazy" guy...

So you'll never get what you actually want.

Look, it's your life. You can be single forever and bang thousands of girls, or you can find the love of your life tomorrow. I can't tell you how to live.

But what I want for you, more than anything, is to have what very few men in this world will ever have - OPTIONS.

And not just 1 or 2 options... but dozens... even hundreds... CRAZY amounts of options, of women you never even thought you could attract... the kind of girls you don't even KNOW you like yet...

And not because you're a sleazy player... but because I think every man and woman should be able to actually CHOOSE who they wanna date instead of doing what everyone else does - taking whatever they can get, and accepting that some people will always be "out of your league."

I want you to take the idea that some girls are "out of your league" and throw it out the window... along with countless other **limited beliefs** that create the **limited reality** you see in front of you now.

And choose to see a life that is overflowing with abundance of all kinds... sex, money, adventure, respect, success, excitement, passion... and yes, above all else, LOVE... for women, for your friends, for the people around you, for yourself...

But first you must look beyond the blog articles, the youtube videos, the cutesy quotes on instagram, the silly little sayings repeated by the mediocre masses of people who don't get it (and never will), the preachy advice from girls who mean well, but who don't understand you as a man...

Look beyond all the noise and confusion about "what women want" and you'll discover a select group of men who have created enormous abundance in their lives.

Men who seem to always get the girl, who always have friends and get invited to parties, who always get the attention and leave with a girl on their arm, no matter what happens or where they are.

These are the kinds of guys you should study and take advice from, not the pretenders, not the PUA fanboys, and not the quitters.

By the way, since you're reading this book, you've clearly decided I'm someone worth listening to.

Thank you!

I appreciate you like you wouldn't believe.

But listen, while I do think you're amazing, I want you to know that I'm not looking for anything serious right now... I also give advice to a LOT of other guys, and I don't wanna teach anyone if they're not cool with that.

You cool with that?

Perfect.

Let's rock and roll...

CHAPTER THREE

"I never have bad days. I have good days, and I have character building days."

That's what my friend Adam Lyons said to me recently.

I rarely pick up the phone anymore, but I always answer if I see Adam calling.

Because I always leave a conversation with Adam feeling BETTER than before we talked.

Even when he's having a bad day, he still has a positive effect on people. Because he refuses to accept it's a bad day.

He chooses to see it as something useful - something that builds character - instead of something negative.

Not by surprise, Adam is one of the most positive, confident, charismatic men I know.

He also has 2 girlfriends (it's a threesome type of relationship) so you can rest assured he's not some "nice guy" who never gets laid. He's a nice guy who is also insanely attractive to women.

You probably know at least one guy in your life like Adam - the kind of guy who gets all the female attention without even trying.

What's their secret?

I'll tell you what it is, but to properly explain it, I need to tell you a story.

This is a story about two guys.

These two guys are walking down the street and talking to each other.

From up ahead, they notice two gorgeous girls.

As the two girls get closer, the two guys wave at them and say hello.

Then, one girl whispers something to the other. Both girls start giggling, and they keep laughing as they walk past the guys.

After they've gone, the 1st guy turns to the 2nd, and says...

"Man, can you believe they had the nerve to laugh at us like that? We didn't hit on them, we weren't being creepy, we weren't looking at their boobs... all we did was say hello, and they laughed at us, like we were nothing. Girls these days are so mean and superficial, they just don't appreciate good guys like us anymore."

Then, the 2nd guy turns to the 1st guy, and says... "Man, what are you talking about? Don't you see what just happened? Those girls LIKED us! They were giggling because they were attracted to us, and we just made them a little nervous... we should go back and talk to them, I'll show you."

"Nope," says the 1st guy. "Don't try to tell me I'm wrong. I know what I saw, and those girls are rude, stuck up bitches."

Which guy is right?

If you think about it, you'll start to realize - they're both right, aren't they?

There was 1 situation... but it was witnessed by 2 different guys, with 2 different ways of thinking.

And those 2 different ways of thinking create 2 different experiences for the rest of the day.

The 1st guy (the negative one) goes about his day feeling put-upon, and victimized. His shoulders sag, his body language shrinks smaller, and he walks around looking down at the ground, like he wants to be in it...

And the next time he meets a girl, he automatically feels fearful, and bitter. He expects to get laughed at again, and he preemptively rejects other women, in order to protect himself from getting hurt.

As a result of this one experience, and how he CHOSE to interpret it... he becomes the most unattractive version of himself.

He chose to see 1 thing... and until he wakes up and changes his way of thinking, **his choice will determine his reality from now on.**

But what about guy number 2?

For the rest of the day, this guy feels great about himself. He walks a little bit taller. His stride is wider, he holds his head up, he smiles and makes eye contact at everyone he sees...

And the next time he meets a girl, he beams confidence and positivity right from the start.

As a result of that one experience and how he CHOSE to interpret it, he becomes the most magnetic, charismatic, attractive version of himself.

And that was just in one day. Imagine how that same pattern plays out over years of their lives... It should be obvious which guy is successful with women and which one isn't, right?

Now, I told you that story so I could tell you this:

You ARE both of those guys. Every man has those two competing voices inside of him - the voices of the two guys in the story.

The man you become is the man you listen to.

Here are some of the things the 1st guy likes to say...

"She's out of your league"

"She's probably a bitch anyways"

"You're not good enough"

"You're too old/short/ugly/fat/broke"

"You don't have anything interesting to say"

"Everyone's laughing at you"

"Hit the gym, fatty. Girls only like guys with six packs and biceps."

"If you approach her, everyone will think you're a creep and they'll hate you"

"You can't do that"

"You're a loser"

"You don't fit in here"

"You're way too nervous, if you try to talk to her, you'll get rejected right away"

"Don't even bother talking to girls until you've had 4 or 5 drinks"

"She definitely has a boyfriend - why even bother talking to a girl if she's already taken?"

Here are some of the things the 2nd guy likes to say...

"She has a boyfriend? No problem! Just be her friend instead, and get her to introduce you to all her hot single girlfriends later."

"Wow, there's so many different people at this bar, I wonder what kind of adventure tonight will bring..."

"That girl clearly has a cool life - you should go find out something interesting about her."

"Is she looking at you? You should go tease her and flirt with her relentlessly until she realizes how fucking cool you are"

"Know what would be fun right now? Go approach that girl and make her feel really good about herself"

"She wasn't into you? No worries, there's always another girl"

"She's being mean to you? Aww, that's adorable. She's so cute when she's mad..."

"It's okay to be nervous, man. Discomfort builds character. Go talk to her anyways"

"You got this!"

"I accept you"

"I forgive you"

"You're awesome"

Are you starting to see how this plays out in your own life?

Are you aware that you have these two competing voices in your head? (no you're not schizophrenic... probably).

Which voice are you listening to more often? And how does your current reality reflect that?

Here's my challenge to you:

From now on, I want you to actively listen to those two voices, and do whatever it takes to turn the volume DOWN on guy #1, and UP on guy #2.

Can't hear the second voice? Many guys go for so long living in fear and scarcity, they forget he's even in there.

But I know for a fact he's in there.

He's the guy who told you that life could be better.

He's the guy who told you to pick up this book.

He's the guy reading these words right now.

Hey man. There you are. Welcome back.

Dude, all you have to do today is turn the volume up on that second guy, and TRUST what he says. Believe him. Follow him. He only wants what's best for you, and for everyone else around you too.

This is the secret of the most confident, charismatic men you know.

And that's the biggest reason my friend Adam gets so much attention.

It's not that he never feels anxious, nervous or self-conscious. It's not that he never has that 1st voice talking to him He's just learned to ignore it and follow the 2nd voice instead.

And if you have a hard time hearing that 2nd voice right now... if you can't hear him at all and you're not even sure he exists...

Then listen to me instead. I'll be your 2nd voice, until you find your own.

Look man, I used to think this kind of advice was "woo woo" nonsense that only spiritual people believed in...

and I'm the last guy you're ever gonna find sitting around a campfire singing Kum-ba-ya or reading "The Secret"

But the truth is, this isn't "woo woo" - it's basic psychology.

Here's a cool psychology trick to make it obvious:

Right now, stop what you're doing, and for the next 20 seconds, look around your environment and take note of everything that is RED.

Count the number of red objects you see. Go.

(count off 20 seconds)

Stop. Now, see if you can answer this question for me...

In your surrounding environment right now, exactly how many objects are BLUE?

You can't answer that, obviously.

Because I told you to look for red objects. You weren't looking for anything blue.

And that, my friend, is the entire point.

You can only ever find what you're actively looking for.

Your brain doesn't notice things until you TELL it to notice them.

So what are you in the habit of noticing? What do you actively look for?

Are you looking for proof that women don't like you? That you're not good enough, not interesting enough, not handsome enough, not tall enough?

If you look for it, you'll surely find it.

But even more importantly... what are you NOT looking for, that you could be if you tried?

What if you looked for something interesting, exciting or unique about everyone you met?

How would that change the way they responded to you?

What if you looked for something interesting about yourself?
What if you went out to a bar right now, that you know is gonna be packed full of attractive women...

And instead of seeking validation from those women...

What if your only goal was to find out which one of them is the best at flirting? Which is the most sarcastic? Which one can actually make you laugh? Which one has the most interesting story to share?

How much more exciting would your dating life be?

Let me tell you from experience - it goes from being a drag, to becoming a constant treasure hunt.

And women go from being "hard to meet" to practically falling out of the sky and into your lap.

That's the power of the "second voice."

Skeptics will say "that's generic nice guy bullshit, it will never work"

But trust me, I know most of those guys, and... they talk a big game, but they never get laid.

That's why they're so uptight and skeptical all the time... ;)

CHAPTER FOUR

One of the reasons guys struggle with women is because they date DOWN to their insecurities and not UP to their potential.

If this is you, then you say things like...

"I need to step my game up"

"I can open any girl but I can't close"

"I can talk to the 7's and 8's but I struggle with the 9's and 10's"

I want to tell you a secret about 9's and 10's - those ridiculously hot women that you *think* are out of your league...

But first, let's start with where YOU are at... not where SHE is at.

Check it out. Let's talk about options.

Specifically, your dating options.

How many dating options do you have right now?

Two? Three? Four?

Because at any given time, the average girl has at least 2 or 3 guys in her "orbit" (i.e. guys talking to her, trying to spend time with her and hoping to get in her pants)

And that's just an AVERAGE girl.

A really hot girl? She's got closer to 10 options right now.

Don't believe me? Get out your phone and get on Tinder.

Come on, don't be coy... I know you have it.

How many tries does it take you to get a match?

Two? Three? Four?

Well, I can guarantee you this.

The really hot girls you see on there?

It takes them exactly ONE swipe right to get a match.

Because every single guy who sees her picture automatically says yes.

Because she's hot.

And she KNOWS this, son!

And it's not just a Tinder thing – that's how it works in the face-to-face world as well.

Every really hot girl knows that she's hot, and knows she has a massive amount of options.

Ever wonder why super-hot girls sometimes seem icy and "hard to get?"

She has TONS of power in the dating pool, because she has so many options.

Pretty much every guy wants her, and now she's sitting pretty.

She's the one in the driver's seat...

She's the one calling the shots...

She's the one deciding whether to text you back or leave you on "read" for eternity...

Why? Because...

Options = Power

Now, want me to tell you that secret?

She doesn't really want to have that power.

It's not congruent to the female gender role to have more sexual power than her man, or to be more dominant, or to be in the lead.

Even if she's a boss CEO who eats men for breakfast in the boardroom... she still wants a guy to lead her and dominate her in the bedroom.

She doesn't want to be on a pedestal.

It doesn't turn her on.

It doesn't give her any passion or pleasure.

It does nothing for her.

That's why she's so damn icy... she's BORED!

Wanna know what she's holding out for?

She's holding out for a guy who has MORE sexual power than she does.

And the fastest way to become that guy is not to study "pickup" or buy a lamborghini or get abs...

The fastest way to become the guy with ALL the sexual power... is to create more OPTIONS for yourself.

Options = Power

When you have options, you always have the power to say "next" and
move on.

You never have to waste your time with mean or conceited girls who think they're too cool for school and don't respect you as a man.

You never have to put up with lame or prudish behavior either.

And because of that, you're more confident, you're more in-demand, and you're less "available"...

Which is why every girl in your life automatically wants you...

(because they always want what they think they can't have)

When you DON'T have options...

... you invest too much time and emotion thinking about women and how HOT they are, instead of thinking about your life and your purpose...

... you're a slave to your own desires, and you let women mistreat you and disrespect you, just because they're hot and you want them...

... you get irrational and angry at hot women because you feel powerless around them – i.e. you reject them before they can reject you.

So look, the dating world can seem really complicated, but it's not when you take a more enlightened perspective.

It's actually very simple.

Options = Power.

When you don't have options, you struggle.

When you do have options, you get what you want.

Want me to 10X your options for you?

Then go to www.singleguyguide.com to join my daily email newsletter, read by thousands of men around the world each day, where you can learn all the best tips, tactics and techniques to create a massive abundance of options in your life.

Oh, and one more thing...

The more powerful you become, the more you'll find certain weak-minded people getting mad at you for no reason...

Some women may also accuse you of being a player...

When that happens, don't be surprised.

It's sad to say this, but some people will resent you for the power you have.

Your power reminds them of how powerless they feel.

It's not your job to concern yourself with their drama.

And trust me, if given the chance, they would gladly trade places with you.

So don't even bother with complainers, martyrs or moral grandstanders.

Just keep on being your powerful, confident, dominant self.

The right people will find you, and the wrong ones will disappear from your life.

CHAPTER FIVE

If you're like most guys, you picked up this book or invested in one of my training programs for a reason:

To get better with women, of course.

But here's where you may go wrong in the process:

You give a woman compliments, <u>hoping it will make her appreciate you more.</u>

Or...

You flirt with a woman, <u>hoping to make her laugh and like you more.</u>

Or...

You try that new "seduction" tactic you learned online, <u>hoping she'll become attracted to you more.</u>

Or...

You treat your girlfriend or wife like a queen and give her everything she wants... <u>hoping it will make her love and accept you more.</u>

Are you starting to see what these examples have in common?

In each one of these scenarios, plus hundreds of others, you are making the same mistake:

You are doing something in the hope that it will make women like you more.

Because if women liked you more, you'd feel better about yourself.

Here's what I want you to understand today:

Most men seek power from outside themselves.

They NEED women to like them in order to feel "okay."

And they base their self-worth on how many women say "yes" to them.

They desperately want to be accepted.

And if women don't accept them - and they don't get what they want - they feel bad.

They feel rejected.

And that's the BIG problem:

As long as you're looking for acceptance, you'll always be afraid of rejection.

That's the bad news.

The good news is...

99.9% of people are in the same boat.

We are ALL afraid of rejection and are anxiously seeking acceptance.

So if you want to be the awesome, cool, radiantly confident man that gets any girl he wants...

You have to become the <u>exception</u> to that rule.

You have to become <u>exceptional</u>.

How? Don't ask to be accepted anymore.

Instead, GIVE people the acceptance they're asking for.

They crave it already - you might as well be the one to give it to them. If not from you, they'll get it from someone else.

Anyways, it's a huge secret to success, with women and in life.

You can't get rejected if you're not asking to be accepted.

Don't go looking for acceptance. Accept yourself, and then offer acceptance to everyone else.

Be a giver, not a taker.

By the way, this is not just good advice you should take - it's an observation of reality.

You wanna get better with girls, friends, social interaction? Well, this is how it works.

And most guys are doing it completely backwards.

Also, most guys suck with women and never get what they want.

Coincidence? I doubt it.

CHAPTER SIX

Have you ever noticed that girls tend to ignore you when you're by yourself, BUT... whenever you're with a girl, OTHER girls suddenly start checking you out?

There's a psychological reason why that happens.

It's a principle called "pre-selection" and it's your ultimate shortcut if you want to be dating hotter girls and having an EASY dating life.

Basically - women are always more attracted to men that OTHER women are already attracted to.

Human beings are funny – we think we're so smart, but we're really just highly evolved monkeys. And one thing you can usually count on is the old cliché – "monkey see, monkey do."

What I mean is, people copy each other all the time.

One guy grows a long beard, and all of a sudden... everyone wants a long beard.

One girl says high-waisted shorts are sexy, and all of a sudden... other girls start wearing them too.

One girl seems to want you... all of a sudden, other girls start wanting you too.

That's the effect of preselection. Use it to your advantage and you will NEVER have to "pick up chicks" again.

I mean, what sounds easier to you – going out with a bunch of dudes and trying to meet women?

OR going out with a bunch of women and trying to meet women?

It's not even close, dude. Date smarter, not harder.

Want to know how I meet so many girls without going out to bars and clubs all the time? Because I have a lot of female friends, and they're always bringing girls around.

Want to know why most guys don't have it so easy? Because they're terrified of being stuck in the "friend-zone," so they miss all their opportunities to form genuine, lasting friendships with women.

They're under the childish illusion that women only exist for the purposes of dating and sex, and if those things are off the table, there's no other reason to know each other. It's really sad, to be honest. Female friends will bring so many amazing things into your life.

Don't get me wrong, you can learn a lot of cool stuff from dating coaches, mentors and advice books (ahem). But none of that will come close to what you learn by spending one hour drinking margaritas with a bunch of women who ONLY see you as a friend. They don't care about impressing you – they'll tell you everything.

And when they hang out with other girls, who do you think is #1 on the "recommended dating list?" You.

So what should you take away from this?

It's simple - if you want to date more women, then make friends with more women.

You meet a girl and she only sees you as a friend? Great, BE HER FRIEND! And then get her to be a good friend back to you, and introduce you to all her hot single friends.

You meet a girl and she's already taken? Cool - meet her boyfriend too and bring them both into your circle of friends.

Remember - abundance always trumps neediness. Where most guys see obstacles, you need to see opportunities.

And once you have a few female friends, get them to help you out...

Tell them to build you up to all their girlfriends - you've got a job, you're single, you're disease free, you're charming and awesome.

Even better - have them tell all their friends that you're trouble, and they should stay far, far away from you... that you're a total bad boy who's always dating a new girl, and every girl seems to want you, but none of them can ever lock you down...

Hell - get her to tell all her friends that your bedroom is constantly emanating female screams of pleasure because you're so well hung and amazing in bed...

The "referrals" I get from having cool female friends are some of the coolest girls I've ever had the pleasure of meeting.

Weak, weird guys are always worried about being caught in the "friend zone."

Meanwhile, I'm in the "friend zone" with dozens of girls, and I've never been happier.

It'll be the same for you, too.

CHAPTER SEVEN

Rule #1 of going out to pick up chicks:

Guys who go out to pick up chicks... don't pick up any chicks!

Why? Because when you're trying to pick up chicks, you're needy. And neediness is repulsive.

The guys who get all the girls don't NEED to get the girls. Their mindset is very different.

To show you what I mean, here are a few distinctions in the right and wrong ways to THINK:

Needy Guy - "What do I say to make those girls like me? I better wait until I have something good enough to say, otherwise I might get rejected."

You - "I wonder if those girls are fun and interesting, or super boring and a waste of time... Let's go find out."

Needy guy - "Let's go to a different bar, the party there is way better"

You - "Let's invite everyone here, because we ARE the party."

Needy guy - "Hey girls... here I am! Watch me demonstrate my value and be super cool..."

You - "Oh hello girls... there YOU are. Tell me all about you."

Make sense?

If you look hungry... you're going to starve.

Change your mindset, change your results.

More:

If your world revolves around women too much, you're liable to make 1 huge mistake and not even realize it:

Showing interest in a girl before she shows interest in you (being too hungry).

Here's why that's a big mistake:

Because attractive women have options. The hotter she is, the more men she has hitting on her every day.

And the moment you show interest in her, and she KNOWS she could have you if she wanted to...

She automatically starts to wonder if she could do better than you...

Girls always want the highest value man they can get - why do you think they chase celebrities and athletes and rappers so much?

But no matter the environment you're in, even in your dirty local pub, girls are always gonna be holding out for their best option.

Obviously, you want her to see YOU as her best option.

But you can't try really hard to prove you're her best option - because that's needy as fuck.

She has to decide for herself.

So the first thing you must do, no matter how you feel about her on the inside, is to play it cool and WITHHOLD interest from her...

Until SHE has shown interest in you first.

Don't get all soft and mushy, telling her she's beautiful and you really like her.

That's not sexy and charming... it's amateur, needy, clingy, and it's only gonna get you rejected or told "let's just be friends."

Girls are usually pretty good at this game... because all they think about all day is relationships.

So when you meet a girl and you really want to win her over, make her fall for you, and even make her your girlfriend...

You have to keep her on her toes in the beginning stages, and never let her know how you feel about her until SHE has confessed her feelings first.

Remember that - always withhold interest until the time is right, even if she's super-hot and perfect and exactly what you want...

That's just how the game is played, and I want you to be a winner.

CHAPTER EIGHT

Here's a quick story and some crucial advice before you start your weekend.

I was talking to 2 different girls last night over text. Both are equally hot in the looks department.

Gabby is an exotic 21 year old latina with sexy librarian glasses, tattoos and big bouncy double-d's.

Marissa is a gorgeous 24 year old redhead you might mistake for a real life version of Jessica Rabbit.

I was setting up dates with both of them, and I noticed something very interesting...

First, Gabby is super excited to hang out with me.

She responds quickly to my texts, she's enthusiastic, funny, clever... we have at least 3 inside jokes now, already.

She's putting in effort. She's showing interest. She's making it fun for me...

But Marissa, the redhead?

I'm not gonna lie, she's ridiculously hot... but she's barely putting in any effort at all.

She responds to my texts... a half an hour after I send them, with only a few words - "haha, sure" - "yeah, we can hang out"

And she's nice and friendly... but in a way that's super nonchalant, with no enthusiasm at all.

The kicker was, when I asked her out for drinks, she said "I don't do drinks, but you can take me out to dinner."

Meh... sorry girl, I don't do dinner dates with girls who aren't even that excited to see me.

Marissa sounds like one of those girls who uses men for free dinners, to be honest.

So I just ignored her... because Gabby is SO much more fun to talk to anyways.

I invited Gabby for drinks tonight and she responded "hell yeah, I'd love to!"

Man, that feels so much better than "no drinks but I'll LET you take me out to dinner."

Easy choice, right?

That's why, last night, I wrote down this mantra on my whiteboard so I'd remember to tell you:

"If it's not a HELL YES, it's a no"

Powerful words to live by.

If you want to instantly improve your dating life, then make sure you choose the right girls, and ignore the wrong ones.

Choose the ones who say "Hell Yes" to you.

Don't just accept a girl because she's hot.

Because some girls, even if they're hot, are just NOT that fun or exciting...

And those girls are gonna cause you problems and leave you confused and unhappy, wondering if you did something wrong...

When the only thing you did wrong was choose the wrong girl.

For example...

It's safe to say that lots of men would EAGERLY say yes to Marissa and take her out to dinner right away... probably pay for everything and give her whatever she wanted...

And HOPE she might possibly grace them with the chance to get inside her pants... maybe, if they try really, really hard and impress her enough with their "game"

Because Marissa is the hottest girl that's ever talked to them, and they are terrified of "blowing their one chance" with her (typical scarcity mindset)

Meanwhile, guys like you and me? We're over here laughing our faces off and enjoying an easy, fun date with girls like Gabby.

And in case you didn't catch this the first time, I must STRESS - both of these girls are equally hot. But one is really fun and down-to-earth, and the other is a stuck-up princess...

Remember that, the next time you meet a hot girl....

Make sure she's a Gabby, not a Marissa... (even if Marissa is really hot and you totally wanna bang her).

Make sure SHE is good enough for YOU, not the other way around.

And don't worry about blowing your chance with a girl - because in your world, there's always another girl.

But there's only ONE of you - which is why she should be worried about blowing HER chance.

That's living powerfully, with abundance.

And I'll leave you with that... because it's happy hour, and Gabby's waiting for me ;-)

Enjoy your weekend, my dude.

CHAPTER NINE

Ever watch one of those predator-prey nature shows on the Discovery channel?

Next time you do, watch the chase scenes carefully.

There's always one or two scenes where the lion or the cheetah is not successful, and each time the scenario is the same.

The predator gets closer to the prey... closer... closer...

But then... she slips back slightly... and IMMEDIATELY gives up. On the spot.

When the distance begins to widen, the predator quits. She walks away, because it doesn't matter. There are other wildebeests, other gazelles.

She (the females do the hunting) will never waste her precious energy on a lost cause.

This is a law of nature, and it works the same way with women and dating.

The men who are the most successful with women? They never waste their time and energy chasing a losing cause.

As soon as a woman starts pulling away from them... enticing them to chase after her... they just stop, dead in their tracks, and move on to the next one.

And that is precisely why most women TURN THE F AROUND and start chasing those men!

So look, if I've said it once I've said it a million times:

Chasing women is a waste of time and it doesn't work.

The more you chase something, the more it will run away from you.

There are always other women. Turn the page on this one. Let her go.

It is absolutely CRUCIAL that you understand - you do not need any one woman.

Because to be needy is to lose control and make bad decisions.

And losing control makes you vulnerable, weak and scared.

Are women attracted to weakness and fear?

Not the good ones...

Overcome neediness, in all its varieties.

CHAPTER TEN

I've been dating a lot of younger girls lately (21-25), and it's taught me a lot about women, sex and life.

My friends and I were discussing this over beers the other day and we formed this theory...

There is a period of time for really attractive girls where everything good happens for them. Usually, between the ages of 18 and 25 (roughly).

During this time, they get everything they want from men, and it sometimes goes to their head (usually depending on how they were raised and whether or not they had a good father).

These girls are super confident, and they often cross the line and act cocky and entitled, <u>because their good</u>

looks give them social power and they know how to use it.

These are the hot girls you see cutting the line at nightclubs and walking in for free... posing on instagram for millions of likes... getting tons of attention and validation thrown at them every second of the day...

They are also young, and kind of inexperienced at life. Everything is new and fun to them...

Most of their life experience has been positive - the world has told them, you're hot, you're important, everyone is nice to you, etc...

BUT...

This only lasts for a number of years, and then they get old enough to realize their good looks (and all the benefits that come with that) won't last forever.

Guys stop treating them like perfect snowflakes... the realities of work and life set in... they have to hit the gym because they can't stay skinny for no effort anymore...

They've probably had their heart broken at least once or twice, and dated one too many assholes who weren't all they were cracked up to be...

Basically, they get older and wiser.

At that point, they either change and grow up... or they get bitter and angry because they aren't the hottest chicks on the block anymore.

And almost always, like clockwork, at this turning point of life, they all say the exact same thing:

"I'm sick of playing games"

Ever heard a girl say that before?

"I'm tired of games, I want something real."

Hell, we've all probably said it...

It seems to be a pretty common part of growing up, for us all.

But I want you to understand this is a huge dilemma for a lot of women!

Society is not as kind to women in the "looks" department as they get older.

Society tells women they are only valuable for their sex appeal.

So as they get older and their looks start to fade, they start getting the message that they aren't valuable anymore.

Some women can't grow past that, and they become bitter and jaded.

And some of them grow up, and realize there's more to life than having big tits and getting into nightclubs.

In that way, it's the same for you - there's more to life than how you look and what other people think of you.

Grow up, and grow deeper. It never ends, and it keeps getting better as long as you keep growing.

You can't change society. So please don't be one of those people who lives in a perpetual victim mindset, constantly demanding that the world changes for them instead of changing yourself to adapt to the world.

Focus on what you can control - yourself.

You can't change the messages you get from society but you can change how you react to them.

You can't control how the wave breaks, only how you ride it.

Anyways, aside from just rambling about chicks and waves, the point I wanna make is THIS:

If the "game" is about how attractive you are... then the wave usually peaks for women very early in life.

But men peak FAR later...

Because our value - the thing that makes us attractive - isn't our looks. It's our confidence, our life experience, our status, our wealth.

And all of those things keep increasing as you get older and keep following your path in life (and keep reading Andrew Ryan newsletters, duh).

That's why guys buy my training programs... because they get it.

They know the value of INVESTING in yourself, so that you never hit your "peak"... so that you're always growing... you're always in your prime.

Keep that in mind...

And if you ever find yourself talking to a super-hot girl who acts way too cocky, don't get bitter about it.

Just understand that she's in that "magic" phase of life where she can do no wrong.

Let her enjoy it. And enjoy her (as long as she's not super rude or mean).

Because she only has a small period of time to enjoy being at her "hot girl" peak...

You have the rest of your life.

CHAPTER ELEVEN

"Fear is the path to the dark side. Fear leads to anger. Anger leads to hate. Hate leads to suffering." - Master Yoda

*Note - this chapter is quite long but I urge you not to skip it.

On the path to improving yourself and your skills with women, there's a light side and a dark side.

And the dark side is very seductive. It's clever. It approaches you as your best friend.

It targets your most painful insecurities. It offers you power in the areas you feel most powerless.

And before you know what happened, it's grabbed you by the brain stem and thrown you down a twisted and corrupt path you're not likely to return from.

Before that happens to you, let me show you a few examples of just how bad it can get...

The Most Hated Man in the World

If you've never heard of Julien Blanc, he's a pickup artist who teaches men how to seduce women.

I don't know him personally, I just know what I saw about him in the news back in 2014.

His seminars were canceled and he was BANNED from the entire country of Australia, because of videos where he shows himself walking up to women in the street and choking them, even when they are clearly scared and uncomfortable...

He also posted videos to youtube of himself teaching this "seduction technique" to a room full of men taking notes.

That same year, Time magazine called him "the most hated man in the world."

He claimed it was all taken out of context and the media wasn't fair to him.

To help you decide what's fair, here are some gems from his twitter feed:

 RSD Julien @RSDJulien · Jan 22
Fuck her, don't fuck her over.

Just Kidding. Fuck her over, too.

↩ ⟲ 15 ★ 28 •••

 **RSD Julien** @RSDJulien · Dec 1
It's a lot easier to treat her like shit if you objectify her first. #JustSoYouKnow

↩ ⟲ 2 ★ 17 •••

 **RSD Julien** @RSDJulien · Nov 29
The hottest women are often the most insecure, so don't forget to treat them like trash.

↩ ⟲ 16 ★ 27 •••

 **RSD Julien** @RSDJulien · Nov 28
Another girl, another infinite amount of lies.

↩ ⟲ 15 ★ 22 •••

RSD Julien @RSDJulien · 7 Aug 2013

Girls will trust anyone... What idiots!

↩ ⟲ 3 ★ 7 ...

 RSD Julien @RSDJulien · Sep 17

Cumming inside girls is actually pretty relaxing when you just give them a fake name and a fake number.

↩ ⟲ 12 ★ 16 ...

 RSD Julien @RSDJulien · 20 Aug 2013

Love is when you emotionally abuse her and she still comes back for more, right?

↩ ⟲ 12 ★ 14 ...

 RSD Julien @RSDJulien · 20 Jul 2013

Sometimes you fuck them, other times you jack off on them.

↩ ⟲ 5 ★ 6 ...

 RSD Julien @RSDJulien · 6 May 2013

Dear girls, could you please save me the effort and roofie your own drink? #JustKidding

↩ ⟲ 7 ★ 6 ...

RSD Julien @RSDJulien · 16 May 2013

No means no. #JustKidding

2   8   •••

RSD Julien @RSDJulien · 25 Apr 2013

I always just assume that any girl who sleeps with me is a slut and any girl who doesn't sleep with me is a cunt.

4   16   •••

To put this in perspective, Julien Blanc has hundreds of thousands of followers around the world... mostly men who are shy with women and want to improve their dating and sex life.

In fact, Julien himself said he used to be a shy, introverted geek who had zero luck with women... the classic story of a nerdy guy who became confident and charming after years of hard work and self improvement.

All the way from "zero" to ~~hero~~ "treat her like shit and objectify her."

But that's just the beginning of this rabbit hole...

Believe it or not, there's actually another pickup artist who was so rapey and violent, even Julien Blanc's company fired him and wanted nothing to do with him...

The Pickup Artist too Sleazy for Pickup Artists

JMULV, aka John Mulvehill, is the pickup artist too sleazy for pickup artists.

His methods are all about crafting a "delusional reality" for yourself, where you are the ultimate sexual prize and its inconceivable that a woman would ever reject you or turn you down...

In 2013, he was arrested for reportedly dragging a girl into his car against her will, and forcing her to touch his dick.

He claimed she was drunk and everything was consensual. She STRONGLY disagreed (and so did her friends).

How do I know all of this? Because it's public record. Google his name and read the news stories. I did, and it took me 3 seconds to find this arrest report:

Name: MULVEHILL, JOHN
Age: 29
Race: White
Sex: Male
Inmate ID: 05991445
Charges:

Case	Charge	Status	Related Case	Arrest Date
13F08642X	OPEN/GROSS LEWDNESS, (1ST)	Active		5/30/2013
13F08642X	COERC W/FORCE OR THREAT OF FORCE	Active		5/30/2013
13F08642X	KIDNAPPING, 1ST DEGREE	Active		5/30/2013

That's right - coercion with threat of force, and first degree kidnapping.

Interestingly enough, John Mulvehill also described himself as a formerly shy, introverted virgin who just wanted to improve himself and get better with women.

Notice how Julien Blanc said the same thing?

And so do most of their followers.

They didn't grow up thinking and acting like predators... they chose that path later in life.

Why? How does that kind of thing happen?

How does a shy, introverted virgin turn into the kind of guy who drags women into his car against their will?

Welcome to the Dark Side

I'm not sharing these stories to gawk at creepy men who do bad things... the news media does plenty of that every day.

I'm sharing this because, as a single guy working on his dating life, you need to understand there is a serious DARK SIDE to the path you're on...

And this rabbit hole goes pretty deep. Don't fall in... but let's approach the edge, and take a good, long look at some of the corrupted men lurking down there...

Harvey Weinstein - former hollywood film producer. Fired from his own company after over 80 women accused him of sexual harassment, assault and rape, triggering the now famous #Metoo social media campaign to encourage abused women to speak up.

"Nice guys"

"Nice guys" use kindness as a way to manipulate their way into a woman's bed. When it doesn't work and they get rejected or told "you're so nice, let's be friends"... they lash out in anger and say hateful, insulting things to the girl.

If you have a hard time understanding why this behavior is wrong, remember this:

Good men are good to everyone. Nice guys are only nice to their "targets."

Go here to learn more about these poor, misunderstood men - https://www.reddit.com/r/niceguys

Incels

Incel is short for "involuntary celibate."

This was a group on Reddit that started out as a bunch of sexually frustrated guys who were upset they couldn't get laid and needed a place to vent.

It eventually became so toxic and hateful, they were kicked off Reddit. If I remember correctly, they were talking about "rules" that society should force women to obey, like being married off at 15, and incest with family members.

Groups also similar to Incels - The Red Pill, and Men Going their own Way (MGTOW).

Basically - a bunch of guys hopelessly addicted to feeling like a victim and lashing out in anger and hate against their "oppressors" (women and society)

And that's just a small sample of guys at various stages of crossing over to the Dark Side...

Now, you may be sitting there thinking, I would never say such bad things about women, I'm not like those other guys. I would never join the dark side...

But you know what? Anakin Skywalker said the exact same thing before he became Darth Vader.

And so did the thousands of men who follow julien blanc, or joined "the red pill" and "men going their own way."

These are usually men who feel powerless and insecure with women.

That's how the dark side seduces you... by appealing to your anger, your insecurity, and your fear.

And it's perfectly normal to feel fear and anger - those are normal human emotions we all go through.

But it's what you choose to do about it that defines you, and defines how the world appears to you.

The first step towards the dark side happens when you choose to focus on your anger, and let it control you.

I know, because that used to be me. Here's a quick story to show you what I mean...

The Path to the Dark Side

When I was a teenager, my mother found pornography in my closet. She was mortified. In her mind, porn promoted violence against women, and she couldn't let me grow up with such evil thoughts in my mind...

So one night at dinner, she brought it out and showed it to my entire family, in order to shame me into never looking at it again...

Imagine your family seeing your most intimate masturbation material, laid out in all its graphic glory on the dinner table, right next to the green beans.

I would rather they all saw me naked. I was so ashamed I wanted to die, or disappear.

And I'm over it now, but looking back, I still feel a familiar twinge of anger bubbling up when I think about it...

How could she humiliate me like that? I was just a normal kid going through puberty, struggling with urges I didn't understand yet, and my own mother treated me like a sexual predator.

It wasn't fair.

Because of incidents like that, I grew up feeling terribly ashamed of my sexual desires...

I was afraid that if women knew what I was really thinking, they would despise me.

Over the years, that **fear gave way to anger.**

I started to resent women for making me feel that way... as if it were somehow their fault.

There would be days when I'd be walking down the street by myself and see an attractive woman passing by... and I would honestly feel ATTACKED by her... like her very presence was a rejection of me.

And of course, when you feel attacked, your natural reaction is to defend yourself.

So I'd fight these imaginary battles and arguments with women in my head all the time.

Can you imagine my insecurity?

As weird as it sounds now... I actually felt like, somehow, women had done me wrong.

And I imagine a lot of women struggle with the same thing - feeling angry at men, in general, because one or two men in the past did them wrong.

But no matter what happened to us in the past, sooner or later...

There comes a point when it's time to take responsibility for our own choices, move beyond our old bullshit and decide for ourselves what kind of men we want to be.

Some people never make it that far, and it's sad.

Those people usually spend their lives playing the perpetual victim, and blaming their issues on everyone else but themselves.

I used to blame women for making me feel scared... but I could have also blamed society, or my parents, or the mainstream media, or Obama, or Trump, or mercury retrograde, or gluten, or any number of things people love to project their failures onto...

All of that is bullshit. Here is the truth:

You always have a choice in life.

Do you choose to be in control, or do you choose to play the victim?

Well, if you decide to play victim, then you're also gonna need something else:

You're gonna need to find a villain who is oppressing you.

On the path to the Dark Side, the villains are usually women and society.

And it won't take long before you forget that you chose to see it like this... and you lose yourself in the victim role, as if it were out of your control...

That's when you'll start to get angry at women for ignoring you and rejecting you... passing you over and sleeping with jerks and assholes, even though you're a real nice guy who would treat her so much better than that...

And it won't be long after that until you decide to lash out and get "revenge" on women... to score one for the nice guys who always finish last...

And you might be pleasantly surprised at how GOOD it feels to pre-emptively reject women before they can reject you...

To say nasty things that hurt women's feelings, just like they've always been hurting yours...

And maybe you'll send a girl a picture of your dick, even though you know she doesn't wanna see it, because women have ignored you for so long that forcing yourself into her mind like that just feels RIGHT... like you're finally taking your power back from the bad guys...

And while you're at it, why not physically force yourself on a girl, because women have denied you sex for so long, that just for once, she fucking OWES this to you...

But it's not because you're a bad guy!

People just don't understand what it's been like for you... they don't understand how women have been doing this to YOU for your entire life...

Who can blame you for being fed up? You have to a right to fight back...

It's only fair...

Because you're the good guy...

Because you've been oppressed...

Because you deserve it...

And if women won't GIVE you what you deserve, then you have no choice but to TAKE it.

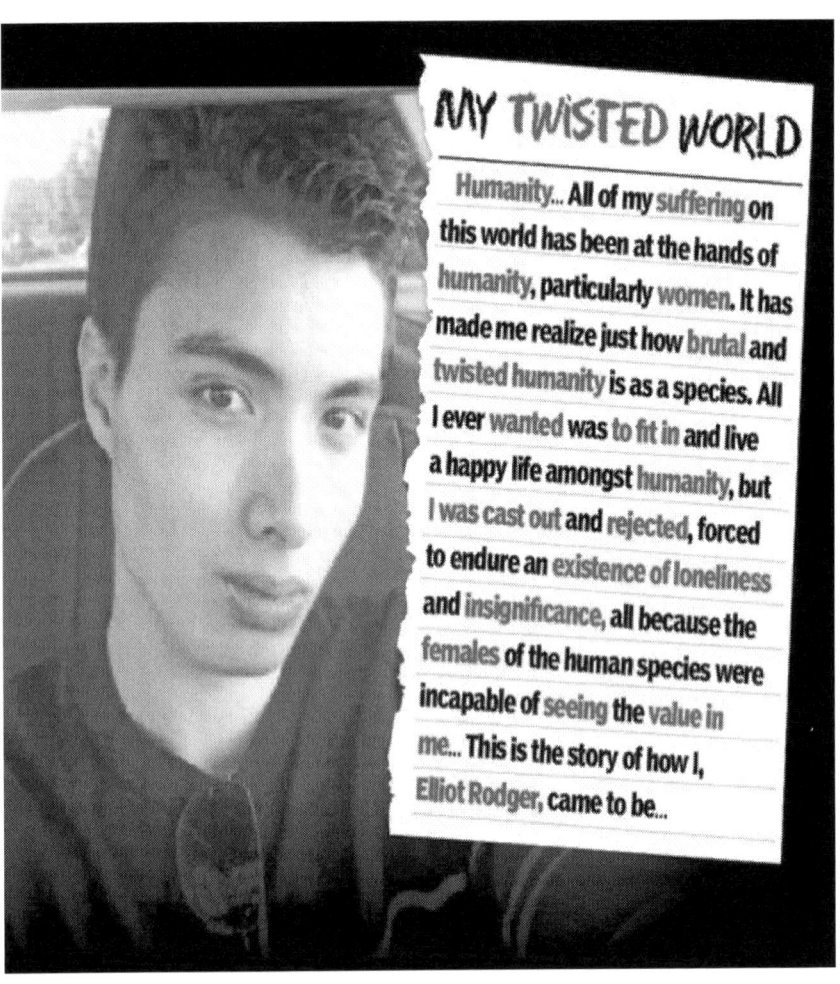

In case you don't know who that is, his name was Elliot Rodgers and he shot and killed 3 women at the University of Santa Barbara because he was tired of girls rejecting him and refusing to see how perfect and nice he was...

He also brutally stabbed 3 men to death - 23, 25 and 94 times - before killing himself.

Yeah, I told you this shit got dark.

Can you see it now? The path to the Dark Side?

Can you start to see how fear leads to anger, hate, and suffering?

Can you see how righteous anger leads to rapey entitlement?

Can you start to understand how some men justify doing awful things to women?

Because they think they have a RIGHT to do it...

They see themselves as persecuted, and they have no choice but to take what is rightfully theirs, what was denied to them by the evil "other"

Anything that separates human beings into "us" vs "them" categories is dangerous.

Anything that dehumanizes the person sitting across from you and makes them into a villain.

That's how people justify doing awful shit to each other.

The Nazis dehumanized Jews and turned them into monsters, because it's easier to shove a monster into an oven than a human being.

In a similar way, the Dark Side turns women into "the enemy."

Or, even worse... it turns women into objects.

That's the deepest, scariest monster at the bottom of this rabbit hole we've been going down...

Where anger turns into hate... and men take pleasure in it... they relish the hate. They get off on the power they feel by turning women into objects.

That's why Julian Blanc was so vilified... why he was kicked out of an entire country for promoting "rape culture"... even though he didn't rape anyone.

Because he promoted the idea that women are less than human... that it's okay to treat them like objects meant for male gratification.

He may or may not be an actual rapist, but he sure as hell thinks like one.

Have you ever thought about that? About how rapists might THINK differently than normal people?

I don't know for sure, but I have to imagine that rapists don't actually think of themselves as rapists.

They don't think to themselves "oh boy, I can't wait to go ruin this woman's life and make her feel violated and terrified forever..."

Because they see women as objects, and you can't rape an object.

An object has no free will. It can't say yes or no. It's there to be owned, used and tossed aside.

RSD Julien @RSDJulien · Dec 1

It's a lot easier to treat her like shit if you objectify her first. #JustSoYouKnow

⟲　↺ 2　★ 17　•••

So now that you see the what the Dark Side does to men, what will you choose to do about it?

My hope is that, once you clearly see the path laid out, you simply choose not to go that way.

And in the next chapter, I'll show you a different way to go…

But first, remember this one thing:

The Dark Side wants you to choose the victim path… it wants you to let fear and anger control how you see the world, and how you see women.

It's crucial to realize <u>you are making a choice.</u> And that choice is mandatory - you have to make it, whether you like it or not.

So you might as well make it consciously instead of having it chosen for you.

The choice is simple. Every day, when you get out of bed, you decide:

What are you going to FOCUS ON?

Because whatever you focus on the most is gonna grow.

Focus on fear, and everyone's your enemy.

Focus on love, and everyone's your friend

That's right, the opposite side of this coin is love.

The Dark Side will try to steer you away from that, by telling you things like...

"Love? That's so corny..."

"That makes you a pussy who gets walked on by women"

"That's weak and feminine."

"Focus on love and you'll be a clingy nice guy who never gets laid"

Haha.

Dude, I couldn't be more excited to prove those statements wrong.

Turn the page, and let's talk about how being a genuinely NICE GUY can actually get you laid like a rockstar...

CHAPTER TWELVE

I'm writing this from my patio right now. It's 9 am. There are three hot girls sleeping in my living room, and one in my bed.

And they all think I'm a real NICE GUY.

Look, this message is for you if you've ever asked "how do I get more girls?"

This is also for you if you've ever wanted to make cooler friends and level up your self confidence, so you get out of bed every day feeling genuinely happy and fulfilled - anything at all that involves getting MORE than you have now.

If you want to GET more from your dating and social life, you have to GIVE more.

Not money and free drinks, not time you don't have, not compliments and flattery...

When I say "give more"... I mean give OF YOURSELF. Give more than is ever expected of you. Go the extra mile for people. And not because you're a nice guy to everyone - because you are a valuable person, and you know you have to GIVE SOME before you can GET SOME.

For example...

Let's say you meet a bunch of girls and you notice one girl in the group that no one's talking to... the one who's probably self-conscious about her looks or her body weight.

"Giving more" means going out of your way to make that girl smile and include her in the conversation.

I'm not saying you should hit on unattractive girls and lead them on... but make sure she's not left out. If you've ever BEEN left out of a conversation, then you know how good it would feel to have someone go out of their way to include you...

For example...

Let's say you see a guy who's acting shy and can't get out of his shell...

Forget your own shyness for a second - this guy needs your help!

Here's what you do - go approach a random girl and say "Hey, I have to introduce you to someone," then take her over to the guy and introduce the two of them, as if you were best friends with them both and they just HAD to meet.

Seriously, I do this all the time - I meet two strangers and introduce them to each other.

It doesn't matter that I don't know either one of them. No one ever asks, or cares... but everyone WINS, and it's because of YOU.

And hey, the guy is super shy, right? So usually, the conversation shifts to you and the girl, and you'll end up getting the girl anyways, because of how cool you were treating them both.

For example...

Let's say you're getting coffee in the morning and you see a girl behind the counter who's worn out from studying and working and making $6 an hour, and she's just going through the motions of another boring, stressful day.

Ask her how work is going. Tell her that her hair looks cute this morning. Tell her she has the nicest smile you've seen all day.

And don't do it because you're hitting on her and you need her to like you more...

Do it because that's just what cool people do for each other.

And hey, maybe next time you come in, she'll remember how you made her feel and she'll wanna give you her number. Happens all the time.

For example...

Let's say you see a group of hot girls trying to have fun at the bar tonight... and maybe they're looking a little defensive against creepy guys coming to hit on them...

Walk straight over with a smile on your face and make their night better because they met you. Ask them if they're celebrating something. Bring the energy level up. Tell a joke and get them laughing.

Play a fun game, and the loser buys shots. Ask them to share the worst pickup line they've heard tonight. Try to guess which one of them is the ringleader, the good one, the biggest troublemaker, the drunken trainwreck, etc...

Yeah, I know, it's classic "being a nice guy" behavior that you were told you should NEVER do... and it's definitely not "super edgy clever high status attraction material"...

But it doesn't matter.

Girls don't care how clever and funny and edgy you are, they just wanna FEEL GOOD around you and let the night take you somewhere exciting together... without feeling like you're chasing them and trying to "get" something from them (notice how our language reflects this with phrases like "GET in her pants" and "TAKE her virginity")

Are you getting this?

If you want to GET some... then GIVE some.

And watch how eagerly girls start chasing you (and running away from the other guys who keep trying to "GET the girls")

Stop asking to be included, and start including others.

Stop worrying about being shy, and help others who are.

Stop wishing people would be cool to you, and start being cool to them.

Stop being reactive and start being proactive.

And do it with everyone, not just hot girls.

I promise you man, this is going to make you feel like a million dollars every day, even if you're a lonely virgin with no self-esteem right now, and you think you'll never feel confident. just TRY it.

Wanna know why most guys don't do things like this? Because they think "other people" can't do anything for them, so why bother. These are usually the same guys complaining that no one ever notices them or does anything for them... this is NOT a coincidence!

if you're complaining that you don't GET any... I guarantee it's because you're not GIVING any.

Wanna know the real secret to approaching hot girls? The one no one ever tells you?

You don't approach hot girls. You approach everyone you're interested in.

Look, if all you do is approach hot girls, what does that SAY about how you value hot girls compared to everyone else?

It says that you put hot girls on a pedestal, doesn't it? And guess what? Hot girls don't date guys who put them on pedestals. Because from all the way up there on that pedestal, all she can do is look DOWN on you.

That's why you get approach anxiety, that's why you think you're shy, that's why you think social interaction is hard... because you're making hot girls into WAY too big a deal, and ignoring the golden opportunities to enjoy other people and LEVEL UP in confidence that are around you all day long.

So look man, if you're stuck in this mode of "omg I have to approach hot girls, I'm so anxious, this is so hard"... just stop. It's not gonna work for you. And start making it a daily habit to interact with more people, just for the sake of the interaction itself.

This is not a tactic or a technique to get you girls. It's a way of living and seeing the world differently. And when you make it a daily habit you will very quickly become charming as f@#k.

When you approach everyone you're interested in, you don't get "approach anxiety" anymore. Your brain switches modes from "omg she's so hot, what do I say, how do I make her like me..." to "oh hey, another interesting person, just like the last 10 people I talked to, I wonder what her story is..."

You shift away from ANXIETY and into CURIOSITY. It's a huge paradigm shift and most guys never do it because they watch too many pickup artist videos and they confuse what I'm talking about with being a watered-down "nice guy" who doesn't get laid.

They say "why would I wanna be a little bitch who acts nice to everyone? Nice guys finish last"

I always find it funny how the guys who talk the most about "what it takes to get laid"... rarely ever get laid... and the guys who bitch and complain the most about being a "nice guy"... are not actually nice people at all.

Remember - good men are good to everyone. Nice guys are only "nice" to their "targets"

You wanna be good with women? Then don't make it about women. Approach everyone you think is interesting, and GIVE more than is ever expected of you.

And don't worry about people taking advantage of you for being nice to them. That's living in fear and scarcity, and it rarely happens anyways.

Don't worry about people taking advantage of you... worry about them MISSING OUT on you.

Worry about them having a worse day because they didn't get to cross paths with you. Consider it your ethical duty to make that girl's day better.

I promise you, if you just adopt this way of thinking for the next few weeks... if you proactively go out into the world and ask "how can I GIVE more of myself today?"...

Your phone will be vibrating itself right off the table with how many texts you're getting from all the cool people and hot girls who wanna be a part of your life and GIVE right back to you.

CHAPTER THIRTEEN

As we grow up and get older, we have a tendency to resist making new friends and just stick with the ones we have.

Some people are your lifelong friends, and you already know who they are.

But the others? Well, some people are only meant to be in one chapter of your story, not the whole thing.

And sometimes, you have to make a decision to get rid of something you don't need in order to MAKE ROOM for what you want.

Here's something nobody wants to admit is true - almost everybody is dissatisfied with their friends.

Everybody wants more out of their social life than what they're getting right now.

If you want to change that, then you have to do what most people are not willing to do…

You have to reach UP for new friends. Not sideways, and not down.

Most people hate it when I say that. They think I'm being arrogant. Well, I think they are being insecure.

Not by surprise, these are the same people complaining about how hard "adulting" is… and they keep living the same unfulfilling routine every weekend, doing the same things with the same people and wondering why nothing ever changes…

These are people who decided, at some point in their life, that they had enough friends and didn't want to make any new ones…

Wanna know why most people don't try to make new friends?

Because they aren't excited about having more friends who are just like the friends they have now…

And that's because they aren't reaching UP for new friends.

But that's exactly what winners do - and that's what you should do too, if you want to change your life FAST.

Make it your goal to hang out with people who are winners... people who support each other, who believe in each other, who challenge you to step up and be better - to stop living life where it's comfortable, and start living life on the edge where it's actually fun and rewarding (and yeah, kind of nerve wracking and scary, which is why you need the support of other winners).

This is especially true for us guys, who tend to keep our feelings to ourselves and put on the mask of "stoic strong guy who knows what he's doing" all the time... even when we're just winging it and have no idea what we're doing.

You gotta hang out with other guys who "get you", dude!

And if you're reading this book, and you're even *slightly* into personal development, then you may have realized... your current friends simply do not care about this stuff like you do.

(don't worry, everyone like us goes through this - it's a rite of passage)

Your friends, family, etc - they don't get it, and you can't make them get it.

They are stuck because they've agreed to be stuck.

Don't try to un-stick them. Unstick yourself and reach UP for new friends.

If you wanna learn some easy ways to start doing that, and join an inner circle of winners, heavy hitters and straight up awesome guys, go here:

www.singleguyguide.com

CHAPTER FOURTEEN

Ever hear someone say "I just don't give a f@#k" ?

Or, "I have zero f@#ks to give" ?

I find that so ironic...

Because if you really didn't give any f@#ks, you wouldn't be saying anything at all.

You'd just be going about your business not giving a f@#k.

That is SO important to recognize if you want to be better with women, and in life.

If you have to SAY it... you aren't it.

But don't get me wrong - being able to TRULY "not give a f@#k" is a great thing.

When you truly don't give a f@#k what people think about you... women LOVE you.

Guys wanna be around you.

And the river of opportunity starts flowing in your direction.

Plus, you're way less stressed and way more FREE...

Free to do whatever you want, talk to whoever you want, say whatever you want, f@#k whoever you want, etc.

There is an INCREDIBLE amount of freedom and peace that comes into your life when you truly have zero f@#ks to give.

So what's the secret?

Don't talk about it... BE about it.

For example...

Instead of trying to impress a girl by being clever, or funny, or entertaining...

Say something YOU think is funny... then sit back and wait to see if SHE can impress YOU.

And if she doesn't... leave and find someone cooler. Because you truly don't give a f@#k if she likes you or not - YOU don't like HER.

Another example...

Instead of reacting to her flakiness and mood swings, and getting all upset that you "screwed things up" and she doesn't like you anymore...

Don't think about her at all. Just worry about yourself.

Work on yourself, and on your confidence - because YOU are more important than any 1 woman.

One more example...

Instead of chasing her and trying to win her back when she stops talking to you...

Forget about her and find another girl. (trust me, she'll come back - they ALWAYS do once you find a new girl).

So there you have it.

If you want to be an attractive badass who TRULY doesn't give a f@#K - then don't talk about it - demonstrate it with your actions.

Now, I want to share a quick story with you, about this weird little teenager who used to dance on the street in this beach town I used to live in…

I've never seen anybody exemplify "Not Giving a F@#K" like this guy did.

Here's the story:

"Wow, that guy is such a WEIRDO."

"Omg I know… he's so AWKWARD."

"Why doesn't he STOP already…?"

That's what all the girls were saying at Waterman's bar in Hermosa Beach, California…

I was sitting out there on a Sunday afternoon, surrounded by pretty girls, sunshine and palm trees.

Who was this "weirdo' everyone was talking about?

He was a scrawny 16 year old boy wearing hand me down sweatpants, a baggy tank top and goofy orange headphones.

Every weekend, for as long as I lived there, this skinny little dude comes to the Hermosa pier.

He puts on his headphones, he stands on top of a 3-foot concrete pillar...

And he practices his dance moves.

For hours.

With thousands of people watching him from the bars, the stores and the beach.

This is FASCINATING to me, for 2 big reasons:

1, He is not a street performer. Nobody is paying him.

Because he is NOT a good dancer.

In his mind, I'm sure he feels like Michael Jackson...

But in reality, he looks more like a drunken gazelle.

Of course, this is because *he's still learning and improving.*

Dancing takes incredible skill and coordination - nobody gets good without thousands of practice hours.

2, This guy is IMMUNE to social pressure. He doesn't care how stupid or awkward he looks, and he doesn't give a F@#k who stares at him.

He just keeps dancing.

Picture that for a second - he could have chosen to practice his dance moves behind closed doors at home, where no one could ever judge him.

Instead, he stands on top of a freaking PEDESTAL, with thousands of people watching and judging...

That takes some serious f@#kin BALLS.

I remember sitting at the bar that one Sunday, listening to these girls make fun of him for looking awkward...

And I suddenly felt angry.

These girls all felt so cocky, sitting there on the patio in their safe little comfort zone, surrounded by people who look the same, act the same and do the same things every weekend.

And they had the nerve to judge this kid for being different...?

Then I realized... it's not their fault. They were just doing what they've been programmed to do, the same as anyone else.

Just like the 99% of people in the world who have NO idea what it means to leave your comfort zone and do something that scares you.

But you and I know differently, don't we?

In our world, that skinny dancing teenager isn't a weirdo...

He's a HERO.

And that's just what happens to people who dance to the sound of their own music - people point fingers and call them weird.

Imagine if every talented person who ever got called weird just stopped trying... where would we be as a society? What great art and music and achievement would we be missing out on?

How smart of this kid to put on headphones while he dances... so he can focus and drown out the haters.

And I guarantee you, he not only becomes a better dancer every single day.

He becomes a better man, as well... because he's not just training his body...

He's training his mind to withstand social pressure, and to stop caring what people think of him.

What would you do if you were immune to the opinions of others? If you had that level of social freedom?

Would you still be living the life you have now, or would you reach for more?

How would your life be different if you felt free to do what you really wanted?

And how would your interactions with WOMEN be different?

I have a strong feeling you'd be dating girls who were *better looking and better for you*, right?

You'd be going for what you truly WANT... instead of settling for what you think you can get.

Everyone says this - we all THINK we want the best out of life...

But do we really? What do our actions say?

For most other guys, they SAY "I Don't Give a F@#k"... but their actions say they definitely DO give LOTS of F@#ks... and they gladly go along with what everyone else does...

Of course, then they're surprised when they get the same thing everyone else gets:

Mediocrity.

A mediocre salary at work.

A mediocre looking body.

Mediocre looking girls.

That's the price of being comfortable and safe, man.

That's the price of sitting on your ass at the bar and judging other people, instead of standing up there on the pier and putting something on the line...

You get a life that isn't BAD... but isn't GREAT either.

It's just... average.

So the question for today is...

Are you okay with being average?

Are you okay with being friendly and safe with women... but never getting the wild, thrilling, passionate experiences you really want?

Are you okay with sleeping with ONLY 7-10 women in your entire lifetime? (that's the average # for most guys)

Are you okay with dating 5's and 6's... and watching the 9's and 10's from a safe distance away...

Or would you rather STEP UP and get better, hotter women in your life?

The kind of women that 99% of men will only ever jerk off to in porn... not because those women are actually harder to get, but because the guys simply never had the balls to try.

The choice is yours:

Be average, or be awesome.

Either sit down with the comfortable crowd at the bar, or stand up and be the guy on the pedestal... dance to the sound of your OWN music... and just accept that a few mediocre people in the crowd are gonna think you're weird...

At least, until you get really fucking good at dancing.

Then they're all gonna want your autograph.

Do epic shit today, my friend.

CHAPTER FIFTEEN

People ask me all the time why I got these tattoos on my hands

They assume I must be a dark, morbid, sad person...

I couldn't disagree with them more. When I think about my life and when it's going to end - and I think about it HONESTLY - I don't feel morbid or sad or depressed.

I feel MOTIVATED. I feel Powerful.

Thinking about DEATH actually makes me feel more ALIVE.

Look man I know it's obvious, and everyone says it... but stay with me here because this is going to solve all your "self-motivation" problems once and for all.

Life doesn't last forever. We all know that. You're here for a while, and then you're not.

And it's not my place to tell you what to believe or what to do about it, but if **you need to get your shit together** then you can't afford to ignore this.

Think about it - when do people ALWAYS get their shit together? Right after they have a brush with death, either their own or a loved one's. I don't think that's a coincidence.

And usually, those people go on to become fantastic success stories, and everyone asks them what the secret is, how they got so motivated, as if that level of passion and drive were not available to us "average humble normal folks."

Are you starting to realize what their "secret" to motivation really is?

The secret is to stop lying to yourself. Stop pretending like you have all the time in the world. You don't. You have right now. Not even tomorrow is guaranteed, not to anyone.

Look, you don't need to have a near-death experience to motivate yourself right now, you just need to stop avoiding the truth and actually look at it.

Go beyond the discomfort and anxiety, and really think about what it's gonna be like when IT happens to you...

What will it be like to die? How will you feel just moments before it happens, when your eyes start to blur and your hands go numb and the world starts to fade away... and you think to yourself, "am I dying? I think this is it, it's finally happening"...

How do you imagine that will actually feel?

And most importantly, what does it make you feel RIGHT NOW?

Right now, you're still here. You're still in the game, baby.

What emotions go through your body when you realize that?

Gratitude? Excitement? Passion?

Because emotion drives action. That's what motivation actually is - a feeling in your body that moves you to DO something.

So what does thinking about DEATH motivate you to do with your LIFE? What does it reveal about what truly matters to you? What does it make you excited for? What adventures do you look forward to in the very near future?

Whatever your feelings are, you might as well follow them and see where they lead.

I mean, what else are you gonna do? Sit at home feeling lonely watching Netflix? Getting drunk with the same people you got drunk with last week, and last year? Watching the same opportunities with the same girls keep slipping through your fingers?

Is that what you were made for?

Yeah, I bet you didn't think a book about dating was gonna get this deep, did you?

Then again, maybe you don't take dating and relationships seriously enough.

Think about this for a second - human beings are SOCIAL animals. That's how we evolved.

Back in our caveman days, we never stood a chance against all the animals out there that wanted to eat us... so we got smart, and we banded together. We formed tribes... communities... all of civilization, really. And still today, we deeply depend on one another for survival.

Social connection is not optional - it's a basic NEED that is permanently wired into your DNA, just like the need to eat food, drink water and have sex.

That's why <u>loneliness</u> feels so crushing. That's why the cruelest punishment for a criminal is putting them in <u>solitary confinement.</u> That's why people hallucinate and see ghosts when they're <u>alone</u> for too long (don't look now but she's right behind you)

We're not made to exist in isolation, brother! We need connection, we need intimacy, we need passion and love and sex and excitement. We need community and family and friends.

And that's why success in your dating and social life is not just a "nice to have" bonus in life...

This should be one of your most urgent priorities.

And you should care about doing it the RIGHT way.

Don't look to the masses for advice. They'll tell you that you're arrogant and ungrateful for trying to become MORE than what you are now.

They'll tell you just to be grateful for the friends you have... to play your role and stay "in your league"... that you can only expect to sleep with 7 women in your lifetime if you're lucky...

Look man, those are average guy goals.

And if "average" = "happy" then therapists wouldn't have jobs, antidepressants wouldn't exist, and people would never choose to numb their feelings with alcohol, drugs and porn.

But those things are the norm, aren't they? Not the exception....

So if you want OUT... then don't let anyone tell you it's okay to be normal.

Strive to become the EXCEPTION to the "norm" - to become EXCEPTIONAL in this area.

That's where all the "gold" is... and that's why you picked up this book.

But before you put this book back down, I need to warn you about one thing.

Did you know... a vast majority of people who buy self-help material never get a result?

That's because changing your thoughts and beliefs takes constant reinforcement. If you've ever read a self-help book and felt motivated, only to wake up a few weeks later still stuck in the same situation with the same problems, then you know this is true.

You need positive reinforcement, man. And accountability. That's the secret of the most successful people who make big time changes in life.

And they don't go it alone like every other half-in, half out, "I'll do it tomorrow" person.

They do it together - with other guys on the same path as them.

If that sounds like a plan to you, then I invite you to join my daily newsletter, which is read by hundreds of thousands of men around the world. Read it every day for guidance and support, and watch how quickly you start to change your way of thinking.

You can subscribe for free at www.singleguyguide.com

I also have a Youtube channel, but that's the watered down pg-13 material.

I only share the "good stuff" in my private newsletter.

It's also the only way you can get access to my advanced training programs, which you can buy whenever you're ready to "level up" certain areas of your life.

These programs are not available to just "anyone" - only my newsletter subscribers and my private circle of affiliates.

Once again, here's where to subscribe, at www.singleguyguide.com

I hope to see your name on that list as soon as possible.

Now, it's time for you to get out there are start leveling-up your life.

And I have a sneaking suspicion your journey is about to lead you to a place full of hot single girls...

So I'll end with one of my favorite toasts, from one single guy to another...

When you go out tonight, try to behave.

If you can't behave, be safe.

And if you can't be safe...

Then name it after me.

Cheers.

Your friend,

Andrew Ryan

Printed in Great Britain
by Amazon

47074920R00080